THE
NEW YORKER
BOOK OF POLITICAL CARTOONS

BLOOMBERG PRESS

PRINCETON

THE
NEW YORKER
BOOK OF POLITICAL CARTOONS

EDITED BY ROBERT MANKOFF

INTRODUCTION BY CHRISTOPHER BUCKLEY

First edition published 2000
1 3 5 7 9 10 8 6 4 2

Library of Congress Cataloging-in-Publication Data

The New Yorker book of political cartoons / edited by Robert Mankoff;
introduction by Christopher Buckley.
    p.   cm.
Includes index.
ISBN 1-57660-080-7 (alk. paper)
    1. United States--Politics and government--Caricatures and cartoons.
2. United States--Politics and government--Caricatures and cartoons.   I. Mankoff, Robert.

E839.5 .N38 2000
320.973'02'07--dc21   00-039836

Book design by LAURIE LOHNE / Design It Communications

THE
NEW YORKER
BOOK OF POLITICAL CARTOONS

BY CHRISTOPHER BUCKLEY

Most people have an absolute all time favorite *New Yorker* cartoon that they came across at some crucial moment in their lives, bearing with it the reassurance that they were not alone in the universe. I still have mine, from twenty years ago. It's faded from sunlight, the back is torn and sticky from a dozen applications of Scotch tape, the top is perforated from push pins as it moved with me from house to house, bulletin board to bulletin board.

I was a lowly White House speech writer at the time, with an office that looked out unimportantly on a sun-deprived courtyard that seemed permanently under construction. My most enduring memory of my brush with power is that of jackhammers.

The chief of staff in my department was a retired four-star admiral, who, though a fine and decent man and a genuine patriot, was—a retired four-star admiral. This is to say, he looked upon New York writer types (hirsute, tie loosened, shoes unpolished, routinely ten minutes late) with a military despair that he was at pains to suppress. And often did not suppress.

Anyway, it fell to Admiral Murphy to vet my prose. Any relationship between editor and writer is a potential minefield. Ours was a federal disaster area waiting to be declared. Once in a speech I quoted the Greek historian Thucydides, causing my principal to become so tongue-tied when he got to the name that he made sounds like John Hurt did in the movie *Alien* just before that horrid thing popped out of his chest. Admiral Murphy came up to me afterwards, red faced and glowering—I was cowering under the table in a fetal position—and poked me in the chest with a naval finger as pointed as a sixteen-inch gun and growled, "Next time say Plato!"

A week or so later, still rubbing the bruise in my sternum, I found the cartoon in that week's *New Yorker.* I had a lovely 700-volt shock of recognition. The drawing was of a politician and his speech writer going over a draft of a speech. The speech writer had the familiar thousand-yard stare of the poor wretch with artistic pretensions who knows—*knows*—that his exquisite couplets are about to be steam-rolled into roadkill.

"O.K.," the politician says, "but change 'Her tawny body glistened beneath the azure sky' to 'National problems demand national solutions.' "

I clipped that cartoon and taped it to my lamp. I would look at it and sigh whenever my beautiful, visionary arpeggios on foreign policy came back from The Committee looking like censored Freedom of Information request documents, along with comments like "Put more here re: historic synergy betw. US and Brazil." The cartoon spoke to me. It whispered, "It's all right; we know."

What a surprise, then, not to find it here! How could such an essential capturing of the relationship between political scribe and client not have made the final cut? The answer is that 110 other political cartoons did, each of them (almost) every bit as good as that one. And all is forgiven, inasmuch as the author of that cartoon was none other than Robert Mankoff, cartoon editor of *The New Yorker* and editor of the present collection.

It was nice, all the same, to find over a half-dozen cartoons about speechwriters and speeches, making that, by my count, the fourth-largest category here. The third largest is Republicans, about which, more in a moment; the second-largest number of cartoons involve the art of spin. The biggest, consisting of twenty-three cartoons is—can you guess?—campaigning, which makes this book all the more timely, appearing as it does in the midst of our quadrennial gladiatorial contest. What a fine anodyne to have on hand as we channel surf through all the electronic bunting and sound bites of the campaign.

Whatever high absurdities and low syllogisms are foisted upon us this time around in the name of getting our votes, it is highly unlikely that they will be as funny, uplifting, or enduring as the moments depicted in this nifty, timeless volume.

We live, happily, at a time when it is more or less safe not to pay too much attention to politics. (How a statement like that must tempt the gods! Quick, let me explain.) Surely this is why the television show *Who Wants To Be A Millionaire?* attracts 23 million viewers while a presidential debate on another channel attracts about one-tenth as many. We can indulge ourselves in this fashion—even to the extent of not voting on election day, as 51 percent of us chose to do in the last general election—confident that we will not wake up on a Wednesday in November to find armored tanks in the street and someone with sunglasses and a mustache standing on the Truman balcony at the White House giving three-hour-long speeches in which he refers to us as "my children." True, we might wake up to find that the Congress has approved $217 billion for a four-lane tunnel connecting North Carolina and Bermuda, or that we now have soldiers stationed in a country no one—not even the CIA—can locate on a map, or that Warren Beatty has been elected president. Such eventualities should be taken seriously, but they are nothing, really, that we can't handle since we seem, one way or the other, to have already been there and done that.

This note of calm is the voice, or, if you want to put a fancy word to it, the ethos—Say Plato, dammit!—of *The New Yorker*'s political cartoons. They are, to the noise and bruit of daily political life, what a zen fountain is to a roaring cataract. They soothe. They make us—liberal, conservative, libertarian, vegetarian—smile in recognition. Yes, that is us they're talking about. How ridiculous we must seem sometimes. And yet . . .

. . .we do care about politics. We may have learned to turn the channel, but often—especially in an election year—they are unavoidable and attractive, even with their Sturm und Drang and junkyard dog nastiness. We become agitated. We argue with each other—with our loved ones!—to the point of fuming and hurling our napkins down on the dinner table like characters in Henry James, while pronouncing each other invincibly ignorant. "You can't seriously mean. . . ."

Between these pages that tone is banished. Sturm becomes a bright sunny day of soothing perspective, Drang is defanged, the junkyard dog becomes a Pekingese, pomposity is deflated, and even the Orwellian machinations of spin doctors—so alarming in real life—appear for what they are: posturings as ridiculous as those in *commedia dell'arte*. On page 68 you'll find a man pleading his case at the Pearly Gates before an unamused-looking St. Peter: "Wait, those weren't lies. That was spin!" I can't wait to show that one to some friends here in Washington, D.C. Maybe it will make them give up their expense accounts and offices on K Street and become missionaries. Hold on, was that a pig just flew by my window?

Distilling all this fury into a tone of gentle wit and piquancy is no small achievement if you consider the antecedents in American political cartooning. The ur-political American cartoonist was, of course, Thomas Nast (1840–1902), whose scathing depictions of William Marcy "Boss" Tweed of New York City's Tammany Hall and of his cronies Peter "Brains" Sweeny, Richard "Slippery Dick" Connolly—why can't more of our politicians have nicknames like that?—helped to bring down Tweed. Tweed is (apocryphally) said to have ordered one of his associates to "Stop them damned pictures ... I don't care what the papers say about me. My constituents can't read, but, damn it, they can see pictures!" Not to press the point, but according to polls, significant numbers of people today get their only political information from Jay Leno and David Letterman.

The Bavarian-born Nast was himself no lovely piece of work. He was fiercely bigoted, a virulent anti-Catholic and Irish-baiter, among his other prejudices. Many of his most celebrated cartoons would stand no chance of being published today in the mainstream press. The Nast-iness that characterized his work was prevalent in much of the other cartooning of the day, which depicted Negroes and Jews and Native Americans in racist caricature that would today appear vile and tasteless. Those days are behind us, but the anger of the American cartoonist lives on. Pick up today's newspaper and look at the editorial cartoon. Pretty rough stuff. Professor Roger A. Fischer's book *Them Damned Pictures* is a catalogue of nineteenth- and twentieth-century visual invective. He includes *Chicago Tribune*'s Jeff MacNelly's revealing comment that "Many cartoonists would be hired assassins if they couldn't draw."

The New Yorker cartoonists may too, deep down, be spitting mad, but they do a good job of transforming that specific anger and disappointment into exquisite generic commentary on the old human condition. The past couple of years of the Clinton-Lewinsky administration have been pretty, er, vivid, and yet I could find only one cartoon out of 110 that specifically referred to the whole sordid mess, and even then it managed to do so with an obliqueness and deftness utterly sublime. You'll find it on page 60. A White House aide is knocking on a door emblazoned with the enormous, great seal of the President of the United States: "Are you decent?" Fifty years from now this cartoon may be more relevant and—to use that inelegant word—accessible than the hundreds of sputtering editorial cartoons that appeared during the Clinton-Lewinsky affair.

If a newspaper editorial cartoon shouts its opinion at you over the scrambled eggs, *The New Yorker* cartoon hands you a Scotch and nudges you toward whatever truth it has in its sights. A candidate for office sticks his head out the phone booth and tells the line of anxious people waiting to use it: "I may be a while. I'm soliciting funds for my re-election campaign." While most of the cartoons here are timeless and general, this particular one may require a little context years from now. But for the time being it is a nice gloss on Vice President Gore's violation of the Pendleton Act of 1883. The cartoon on page 35 might also need some explaining down the line. A crowd is gathered around an ambulance at the scene of an accident. "Let me through," declares a businesslike-looking man holding a briefcase, "I'm a compassionate conservative." I'm dying to ask the cartoonist, Mick Stevens, what's in the briefcase? A health insurance waiver? A legally-concealed handgun with which to finish off the poor victim?

Which brings up the question, why do Republican-oriented cartoons here outnumber Democrat ones by five to one? The answer is simple enough that even someone with a C average from Yale—or from Harvard, for that matter—could figure it out. As objects of fun Republicans just plain make better targets than Democrats; likewise conservatives over liberals. I say this as a card-carrying, faithful (if often despairing), member of the Republican party. In fact, I'm proud of us for being funnier than Democrats. What's it claimed that Oscar Wilde said about the trouble with socialism? Takes too many evenings. Muffy! Where's that blasted new butler put my martini shaker?

Maybe this will change as the old stereotypes continue to evolve. So many of my liberal friends have begun developing rather French tendencies ("Think Left, live Right"). Maybe they'll even take up whaling. Anyway, until someone produces a Ph.D. thesis on the subject, there's my explanation for why there are ten cartoons about Republicans, only two about Democrats.

In the end, it's the *New Yorker* cartoonists, not the jabbering TV talking heads or pundits or spin doctors, who are the true gnostics of American politics, the keepers and tellers of its deepest truths. To the poor candidates, I can only say: After your death you were better have a bad epitaph than their ill report while you live. (No, that's not ungrammatical—it's from *Hamlet*.)

Let's close with a couple of greatest hits:

The candidate standing at the podium with grin and open arms: "People of North Dakota! Or possibly South Dakota!"

The angry congressman standing at his desk in the chamber, replying to his distinguished colleague: "Listen, pal! I didn't spend seven million bucks to get here so I could yield the floor to you."

The two aides looking on in horror at their candidate, as he addresses a large crowd of very displeased-looking people. "Good God! He's giving the white-collar voters' speech to the blue-collars!"

One more for the road? If by election time you find yourself despairing and in a Melvillian, damp, drizzly November-of-the-soul frame of mind, just open this book to page 107 where you'll find a senator or congressman at his desk, scowling at the secretary who has just entered carrying a coat: "No, no, Miss Clark! I asked you to bring in the Mantle of Greatness, not the Cloak of Secrecy."

See—it's still a great country. Don't you feel better now?

"*In the midst of chaos, Larry is the clear voice of reason. Get him the hell out of here.*"

"I'm undecided, but that doesn't mean I'm
apathetic or uninformed."

"Say, who the hell's been writing this stuff?
It comes perilously close to the truth."

*"It was either the knish in Coney Island, the cannoli in Little Italy,
or that divinity fudge in Westchester."*

"*Senator, the American people, whom you often mention in your speeches, would like a word with you.*"

*"My alcohol intake has more than doubled over the last four years,
and the President has done precious little to prevent it."*

"That's an excellent prescreened question, but before I give you my stock answer I'd like to try to disarm everyone with a carefully rehearsed joke."

"I may be awhile. I'm soliciting funds for my reëlection campaign."

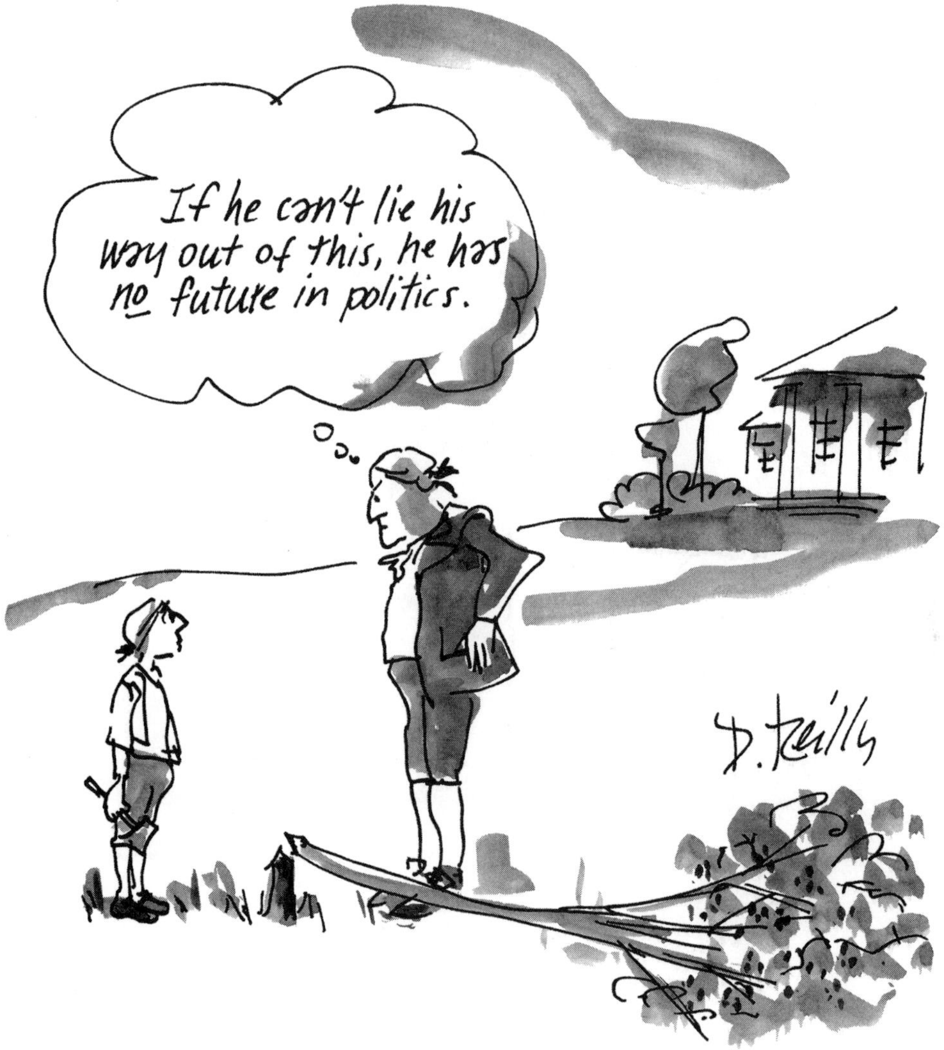
If he can't lie his way out of this, he has no future in politics.
D. Reilly

"Yes, son, we're Republicans."

"Finally, let me put to rest the so-called 'character' issue."

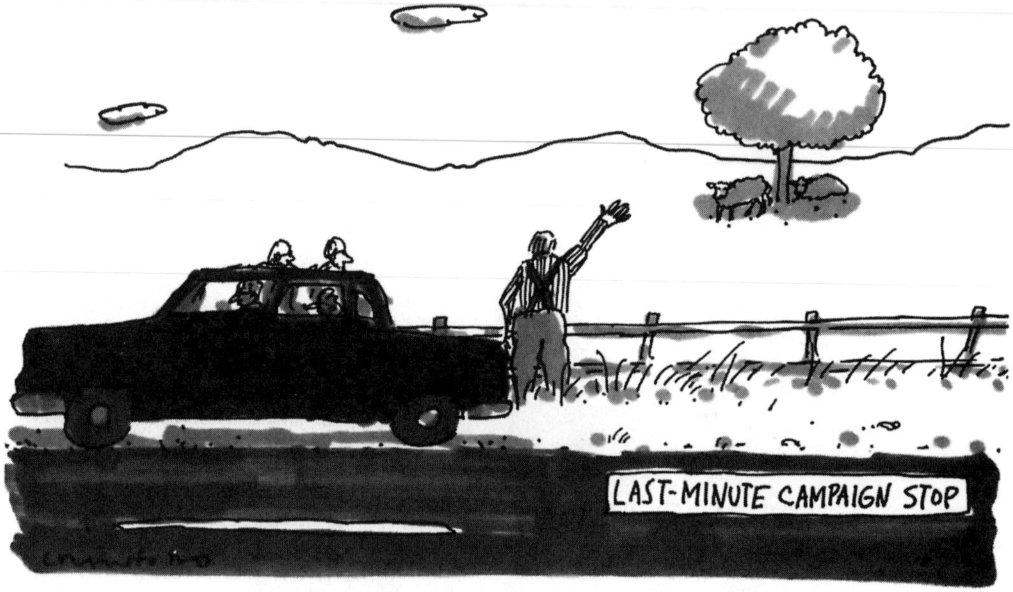
LAST-MINUTE CAMPAIGN STOP

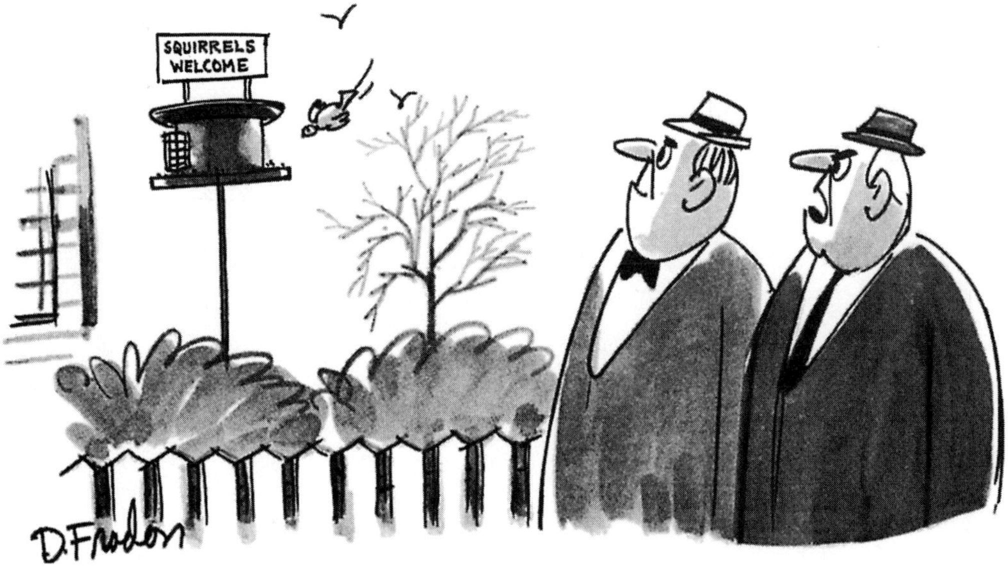
SQUIRRELS
WELCOME
D.Fradon

"Liberals!"

"If indicted, I will not stand trial; if convicted,
I will not serve time."

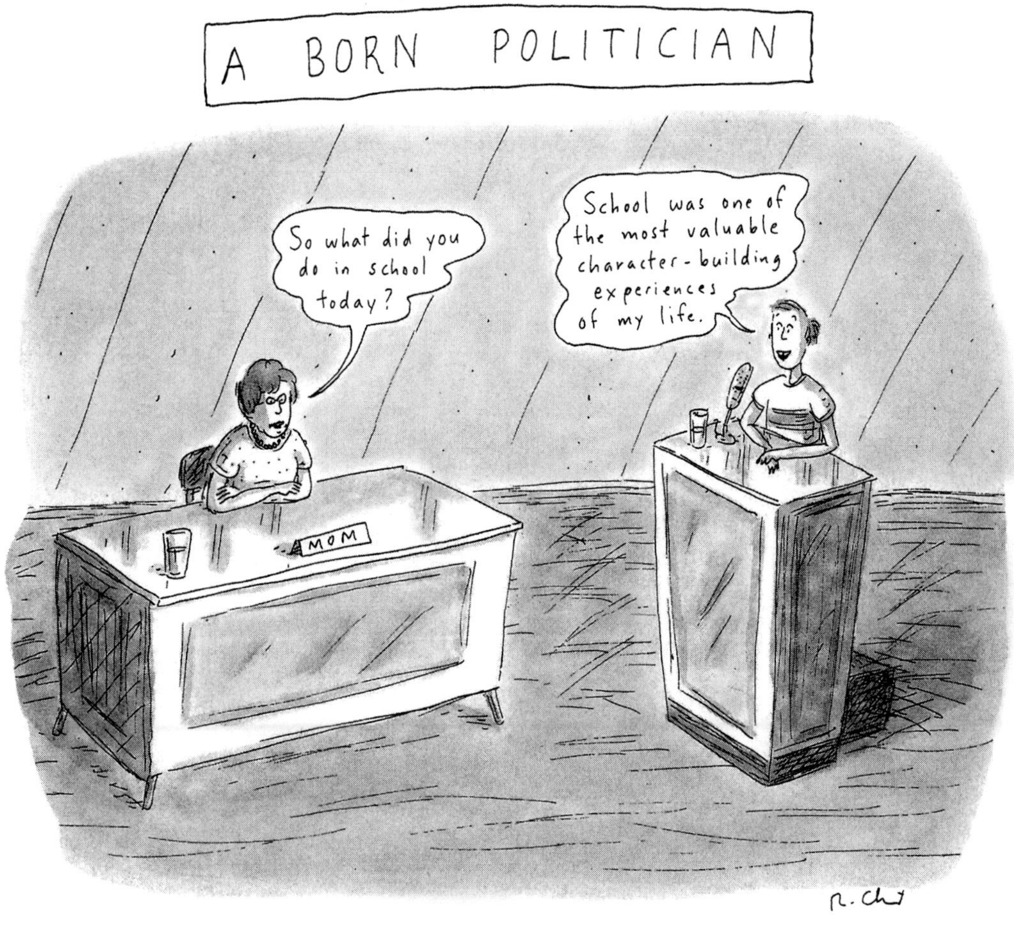
A BORN POLITICIAN
So what did you do in school today?
School was one of the most valuable character-building experiences of my life.
MOM
R. Chst

"*Before I became a black conservative, I was a white liberal.*"

*"If you are a Democrat, Mrs. Hooper-Smith
does the Macarena during your pancakes."*

FB Modell

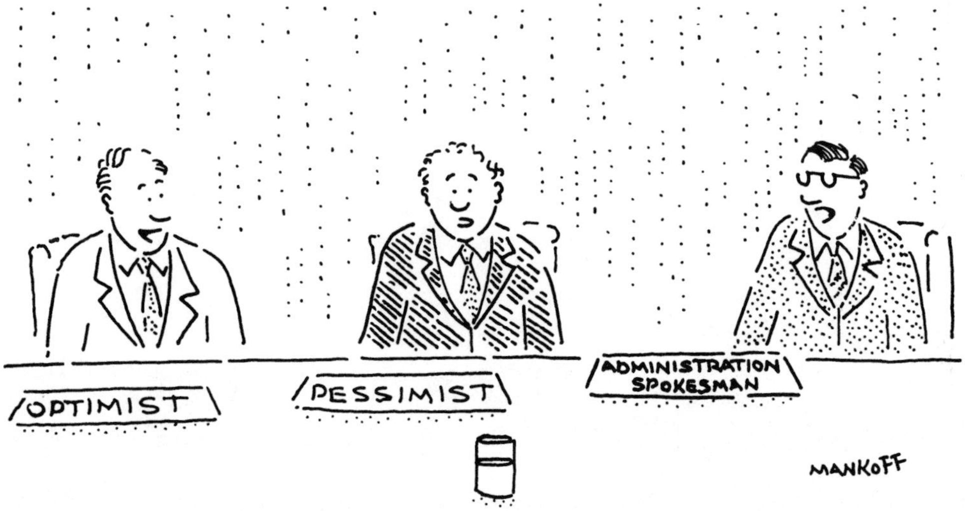
OPTIMIST
PESSIMIST
ADMINISTRATION SPOKESMAN
MANKOFF

"Half full."

"Half empty."

"Half empty because of congressional inaction, and half full because of the tireless efforts of the President."

"Say! I've got a great idea for a dark horse—me!"

"I liked Ike, period."

"As I said earlier, Michelle, I won't answer questions about economic
or foreign policy. I'm here to talk about my sexual escapades."

"People of North Dakota! Or possibly South Dakota!"

"Who's our representative?"

"I have a brief statement, a clarification, and two denials."

AIR TEMP. 92°
WATER TEMP. 78°
WIND S.W. 6 M.P.H.
SUNBURN INDEX 8
OVERNIGHT
CHANGE
IN THE
PRESIDENT'S
APPROVAL
RATING
-2%

"If I become President, I'm not giving any of _my_ schoolfriends jobs."

"Yet _another_ bipartisan commission!"

"What I want is an address that speaks with one voice."

"I'd like to stall this project into the ground—hand it over to one of our action committees."

"First political cartoonist I've ever seen who draws from live models."

"Election Day is dawning, and I'm still undecided."

"I may run, but first I want to toy with the electorate for a while."

"I love this place—its food, its ambience, and its political goals."

"*Let me through. I'm a compassionate conservative.*"

"On the other hand, if we backpedal too much, we'll lose the hate vote."

"I suppose we'll have to set this down as a doubtful district."

"Come now, folks, this baby _must_ belong to one of you."

"It's nothing like that, Annie. I just want to start seeing women from other swing states for a while."

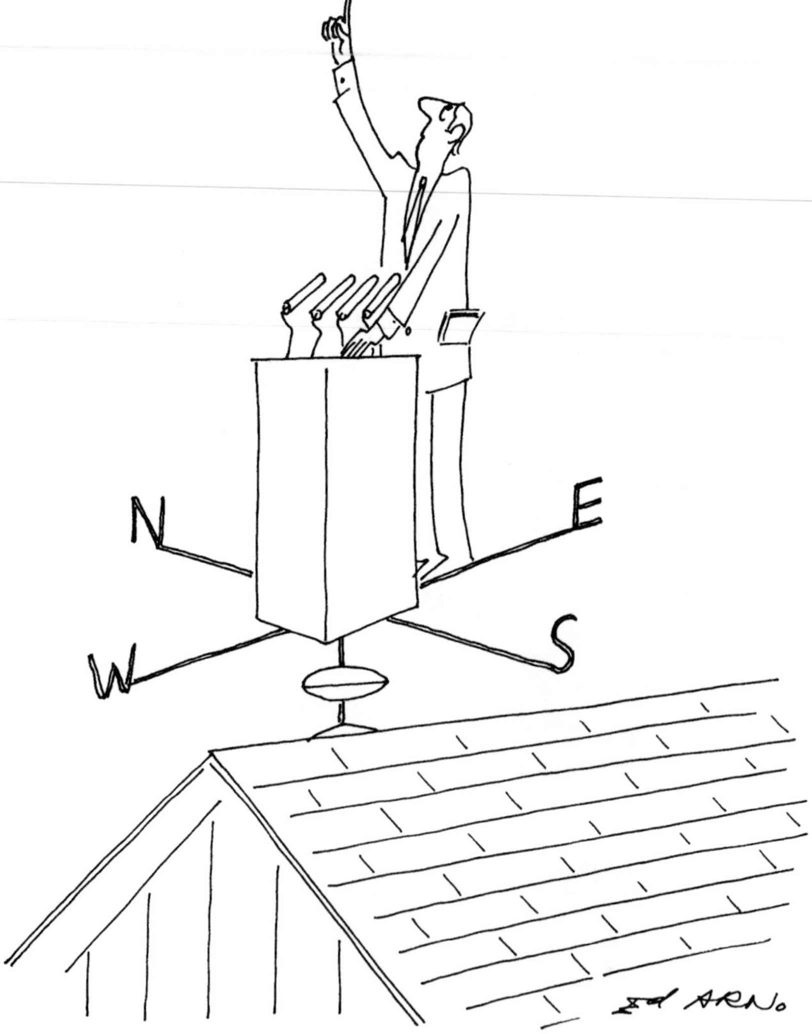
N
E
S
W
Ed Arno

"Listen, pal! I didn't spend seven million bucks to get here so I could yield the floor to you."

"The question is: Which of his irritating mannerisms can be used to political advantage?"

"Very Republican. I love it."

"And now, if you don't mind, I would like to reassess my position
on the firm stand I took in my previous reassessment."

"Our panel today includes Hurley Throod, the opinionated Washington bureau chief; Dennis Wurtner, the lightweight TV commentator; Marsha Boyle, the contentious syndicated columnist; and Sidney H. Hall, the self-styled political expert."

"*You know you have my support on pork and beans, but where do you stand on chicken and dumplings?*"

"*Good God! He's giving the white-collar voters' speech to the blue collars.*"

"Bad news—that fire in your belly is an ulcer."

"It *is* a superb vision of America, all right, but I can't remember which candidate projected it."

"Simply put, Marcia, I want to be your President."

"You've been around here longer than I have. What <u>are</u> 'congressional ethics'?"

"On the left is Senator Binghamton, giving his views, and on the right is Mr. Plimpton, his aide, echoing those views."

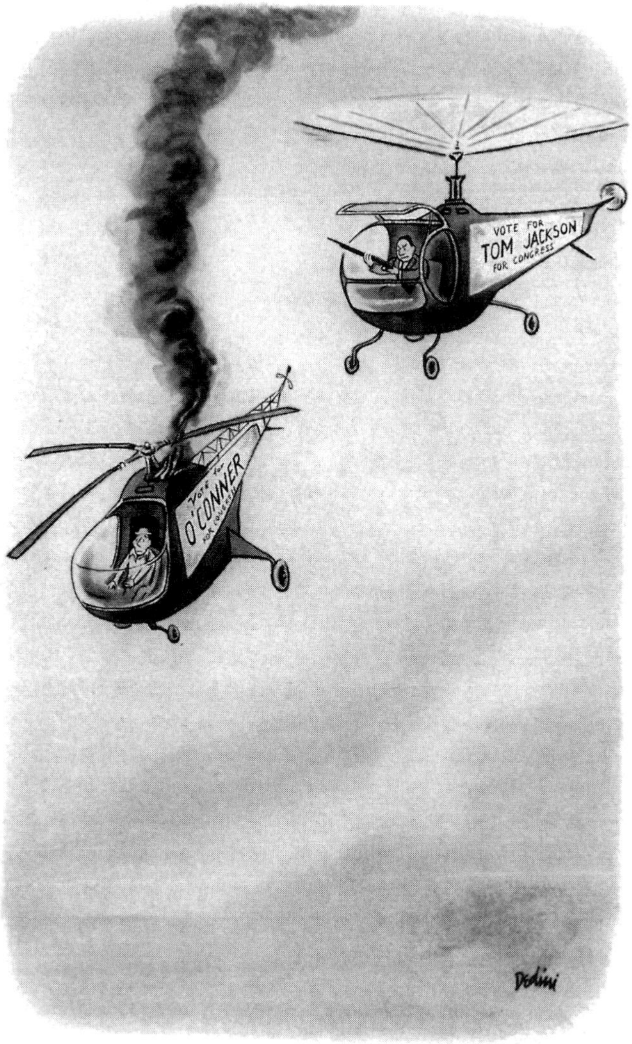
VOTE FOR
TOM JACKSON
FOR CONGRESS
O'CONNER
Dedini

"Take this, Henderson, and hide it from the public."

"Gee, I haven't seen you since that McGovern rally
in '72. You were wearing a cartridge belt."

Keynote Address

Seconding Speech

Platform

Split Delegation

Coalition Candidate

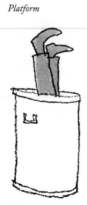

Early Drive Fails

Bandwagon

Kingmaker

Releasing Delegates

Caucus

Farm Bloc

Favorite Son

Balanced Ticket

Steamroller

"Oh my, everybody you mentioned would make a <u>great</u> President."

"But, Ed, that's the ad game. One day you're in the political arena and the next day you're selling detergents."

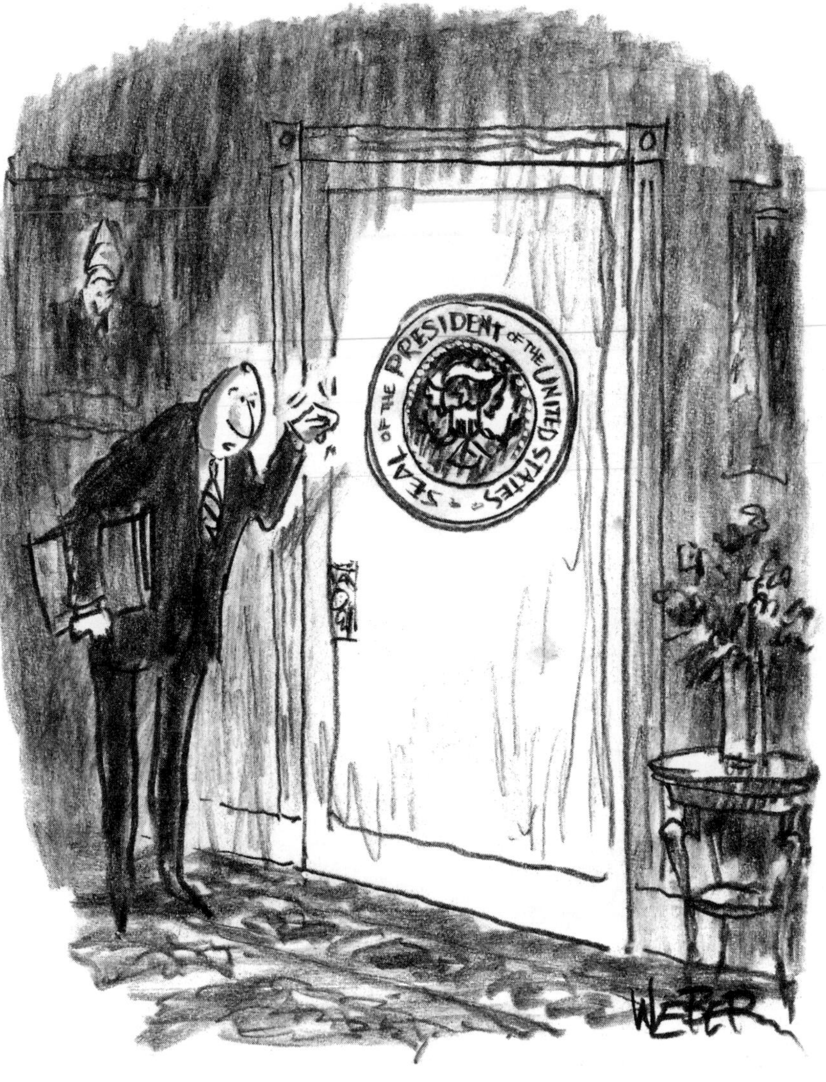
SEAL OF THE PRESIDENT OF THE UNITED STATES
WEBER

"Are you decent?"

LONG AFTER LOSING THE ELECTION, FRED GORT CONTINUED TO CAMPAIGN, THUS MAKING A MOCKERY OF THOSE REPORTERS WHO HAD LABELLED HIM "THE I-DON'T-CARE CANDIDATE."

"All too human is fine—unless, of course, it's all too often."

"Sorry, boys. I was told to keep my big mouth shut."

"*No one comes close to him for sound bites!*"

"A well-regulated militia being necessary to the security of
a free state, we need cheap, available handguns."

"If we lose this district by just two votes, God help you!"

*"Mr. Speaker, will the gentleman from Small Firearms
yield the floor to the gentleman from Big Tobacco?"*

"'Wait, those weren't lies. That was spin!'"

"Someday, son, all my campaign funds will be yours."

AN **OUTSIDER-PARTY** CANDIDATE IS FORCED TO ADMIT THAT HE ONCE VISITED WASHINGTON, D.C.

"With the Suzuki method, they start them campaigning as early as three or four."

"On the other hand, it's great to be out of Washington!"

"Your constant cries to cut the pork sadden me, Senator."

*"The main body of this Inaugural Address is great,
but he wants a happier ending."*

"Good morning. I'm Craig Nisbet, and I'm
trying to meet women."

"My God! I went to sleep a Democrat and I've awakened a Republican."

"Congratulations, Dave! I don't think I've read a more beautifully evasive and subtly misleading public statement in all my years in government."

*"My heartfelt thanks to Kitty Lundell for writing my speeches,
and to Keith Donegan for delivering them."*

"I don't think you can distance yourself from the White House on this one. After all, you __are__ the President."

"You know what I like about power? It's so damn empowering."

"You don't look as if you voted."

"I made a bid for the Senate, but this is as far as I got."

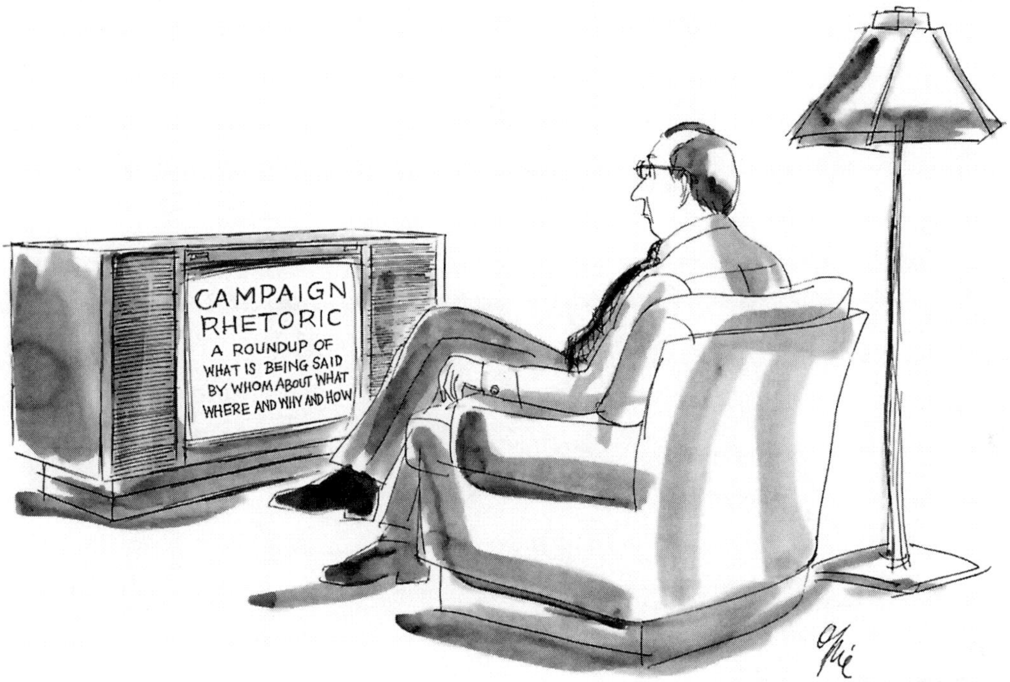
CAMPAIGN
RHETORIC
A ROUNDUP OF
WHAT IS BEING SAID
BY WHOM ABOUT WHAT
WHERE AND WHY AND HOW

"*Excuse me, Senator, but isn't that the same tune
the Administration's been singing?*"

"Aw, come on, guys! We've marketed worse candidates!"

"Callahan, get off my coattails!"

"You're doing better, dear. In
the last election, you conceded much earlier."

"No, no, Senator, no thanks are necessary at this time."

"*You can't legislate morality, thank heaven.*"

"I bet you're glad you got out of politics to spend more time with your family."

"Grayson is a liberal in social matters, a conservative in economic matters, and a homicidal psychopath in political matters."

"*And every time I start to get the least bit serious about a Republican he turns out to be a Log Cabin Republican.*"

POLITICAL CANDIDATES' PLAYBOOK

SIGNALS FROM THE SIDELINES

DO A FLIP-FLOP.

OPPOSE CRIME.

SOFT-PEDAL THE ISSUE.

WAVE THE FLAG.

EMPHASIZE FAMILY VALUES.

POINT THE FINGER.

INVOKE GOD.

STEVENSON

"*This guy's organ-donor card specifies 'For any deserving conservative.'*"

"All right, I lied to you. __All__ governments lie!"

*"Great. You've touched all the bases without getting
bogged down in constitutionality."*

"There's not a dime's worth of difference between the candidates.
They're both carnivores."

IN RATHER THAN OUT

OUT RATHER THAN IN

"And today in Washington a top Administration apologist issued an apology while denying that there was anything to apologize for."

"I'll go out on a limb and say time will tell."

"And as the campaign heats up, the latest poll shows the Dan Rather news team running slightly ahead of the Peter Jennings news team, with the Tom Brokaw team just two points back and gaining."

"So essentially what you're saying is that Joe Sixpack and
Joe Blow are one and the same person?"

"And if I'm elected I promise to go with the flow."

"And so, due to the appearance of wrongdoing, I've decided to simulate my resignation."

"*I want everybody to shake hands with some of the cleanest money in our whole campaign.*"

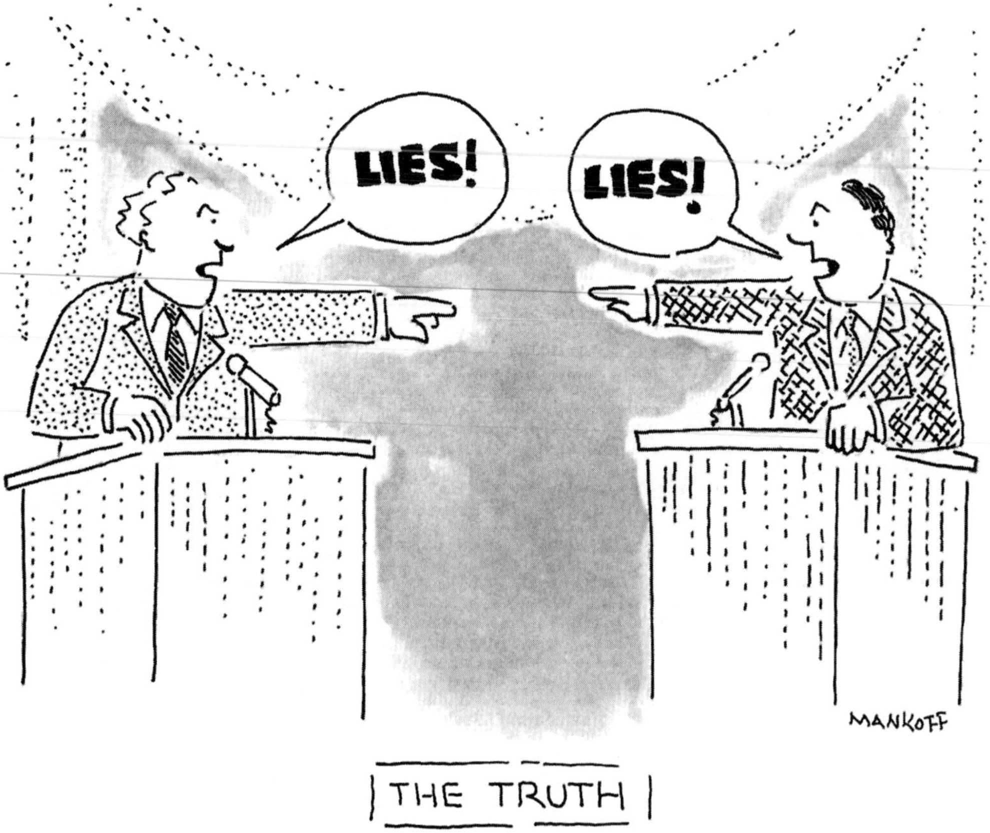
LIES!
LIES!
THE TRUTH
MANKOFF

"No, no, Miss Clark! I asked you to bring in the Mantle of
Greatness, not the Cloak of Secrecy."

"We'll probably vote for the least qualified candidate. We have no judgment skills."

"*I think Republicans and Democrats alike can agree that Frank Shustermann is dead.*"

"It's the end of another campaign day, dear. Any closing statements?"

INDEX OF ARTISTS